SERGEI PROKOFIEV

SONATA FOR VIOLIN SOLO (Op. 115)

Boosey & Hawkes, Music Publishers Ltd.
for Great Britain and British Commonwealth of Nations (except Canada)

Le Chant du Monde, Paris
pour la France, Belgique, Luxembourg et les Pays francophones de l'Afrique

Japan-Soviet Music Inc., Tokyo
for Japan

G. Ricordi & C., Milano
per l'Italia

Musikverlag Hans Sikorski, Hamburg
für die Bundesrepublik Deutschland einschl. West-Berlin, Griechenland, Israel,
Niederlande, Portugal, Schweiz, alle skandinavischen Länder (ohne Finnland),
Spanien und Türkei

Edition Fazer, Helsinki
for Finland

ED 3361

ISBN 0-7935-7421-8

G. SCHIRMER, Inc.

DISTRIBUTED BY

7777 W. BLUEMOUND RD. P.O. BOX 13819 MILWAUKEE, WI 53213

Sonata for Violin Solo, Op. 115

I

Sergei Prokofiev (1947)

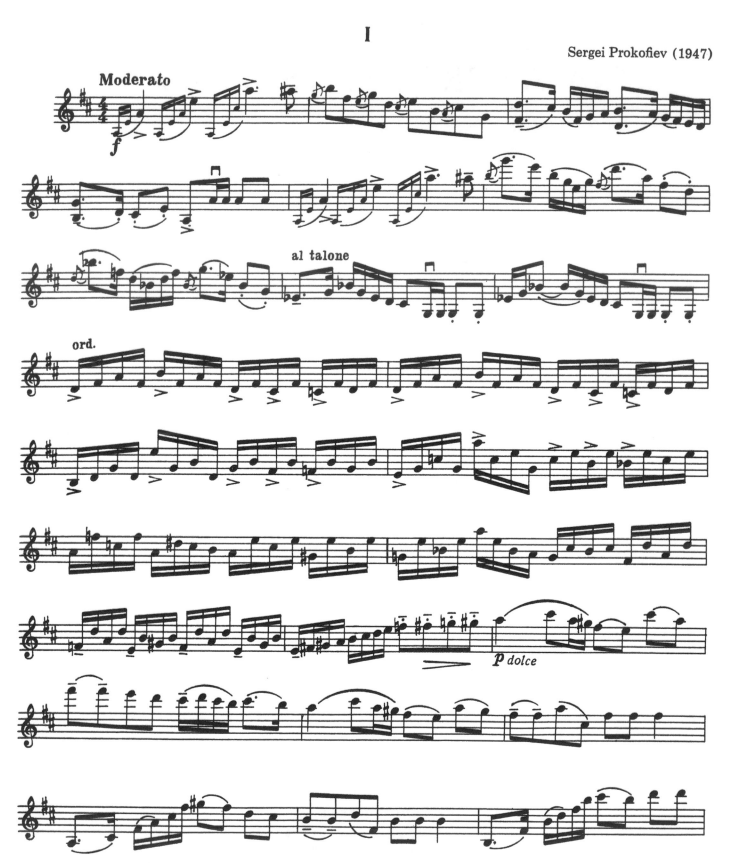

48292c

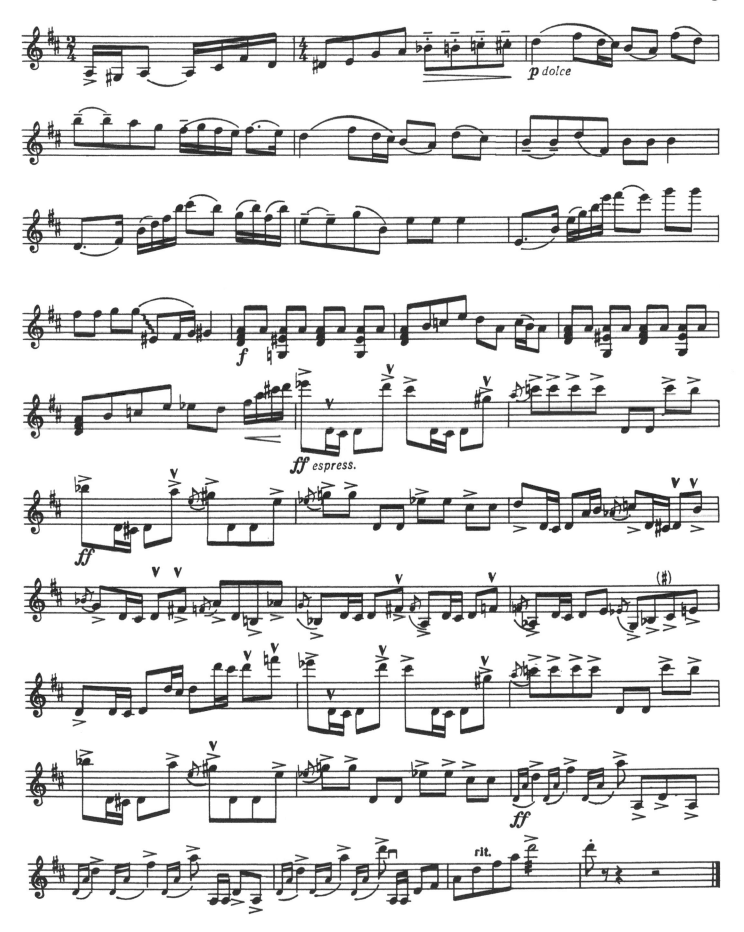

II

Andante dolce

Allegro precipitato

Tempo I